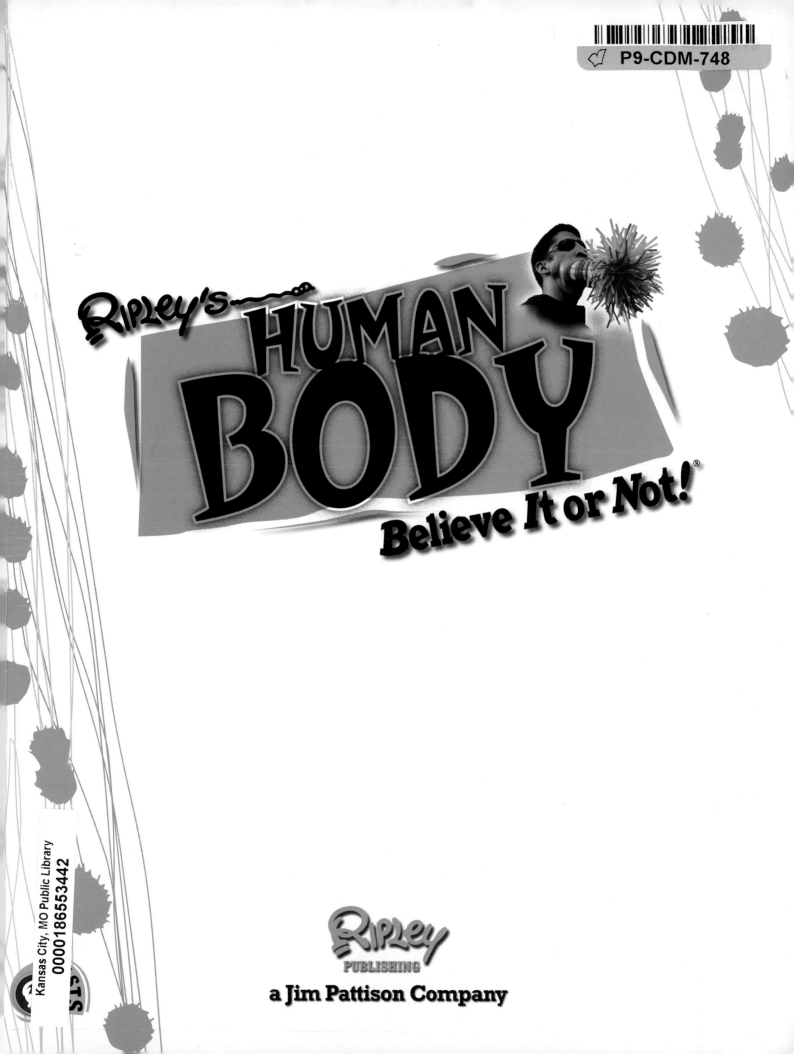

Ripley's HUMAN BODY

Believe It or Not!®

RIPLEY
PUBLISHING

a Jim Pattison Company

Written by Camilla de la Bedoyere
Consultant Dr. Irfan Ghani

RIPLEY
PUBLISHING

Publisher Anne Marshall

Managing Editor Rebecca Miles Picture Researcher James Proud Editors Lisa Regan, Rosie Alexander Assistant Editor Amy Harrison Proofreader Judy Barratt Indexer Hilary Bird

Art Director Sam South
Design Rocket Design (East Anglia) Ltd
Reprographics Stephan Davis

www.ripleys.com/books

Contents

PAGE 8

TWISTS

PAGE 7

Body Beautiful

>> it's all about you >>

The human body is an amazing creation. A collection of bones, blood and other vital bits, your body is just brilliant. There's so much going on inside your head and under your skin – things you know about, like doing your homework and eating your tea, and things you don't even have to think about, like breathing, bending and going to the loo.

This book will take you on a guided tour of the things that make you tick. Get to grips with how your muscles work, take a look inside an eyeball, and think about your brain and everything it does on a daily basis. Each page will open your eyes to the fantastic things going on in the human body, with special Ripley's fascinating facts and amazing 'Believe It or Not!' stories from around the world. What are you waiting for? Get stuck in!

The spine is made up of lots of odd-shaped bones called vertebrae (say ver-tuh-bray).

There is a hole in the middle of each vertebra, which the spinal cord fits through.

Each year, nearly 7 million people in the US are treated for a broken bone.

The ribs form a protective cage (literally called the ribcage) around vital organs such as the heart and lungs. Most people have 12 pairs of ribs, making 24 altogether, but some people are born with only 11 pairs, and others get an extra rib or two!

EPIDERMIS
The top layer of your skin is called the epidermis. It is made from dead cells that are shed every 27 days.

Found a new word? Big word alerts will explain it for you.

Learn fab fast facts to go with the cool pictures.

It's Alimentary
>>digestion>>

Your digestive system is a fabulous food processor. It pulps and pulverises food before squirting it with burning acids and churning it into a stinking stomach soup that is forced through your gurgling guts (also known as intestines).

Billions of bacteria break the food down into smaller and smaller bits so they can be used to fuel your body and help it grow.

A sandwich's journey through your alimentary canal – from mouth to anus – can take more than 24 hours and covers around 7 m in total.

KEY FACTS

Your **alimentary canal** is packed with chemicals called enzymes. These powerful juices help break food down into useful nutrients.

The **oesophagus** is a tube that leads from your mouth to your stomach. It's made of muscles that force the food downwards.

Your **gall bladder** and **pancreas** store and produce substances that help the body's digestive process.

After a big meal your stomach can stretch to **40 times** the size it was when it was empty.

One type of bacteria – **Heliobacter pylori** - survives in the stomach's burning juices. These mini-bugs infect half of the world's people, and can cause pain and ulcers.

Oesophagus

Stomach

Gall bladder

Pancreas

It's big!

The small intestine is lined with tiny, finger-like villi. On the surface of the villi are even tinier folds called microvilli. If you stretched all your villi out they would cover an entire football field!

Believe It or Not!

This rice cracker contains digger wasps! They are a delicacy specially created for the Japanese fan club for wasps.

TASTY!

Appendix

Anus

Small intestine (ileum)

Large intestine (colon)

Twists are all about Believe It or Not: amazing facts, feats, and things that will make you go 'Wow!'.

Do the twist

This book is packed with incredible facts about the human body. It will teach you amazing things about your body, but like all Twists books, it shines a spotlight on things that are unbelievable but true. Turn the pages and find out more...

...bicycles, televisions, and even aircraft with no problems! He has to take them apart and slurp down mineral oil before swallowing the smaller bits.

garbage collection ...Farook, from Tirunelveli, ...eating nothing but flies.

LIVE TREE FROGS AND RATS
For over 40 years, Jiang Musheng of China has eaten live tree frogs and rats to ward off abdominal pains.

CHICKEN FEED
Jan Csovary, from Prievidza, Slovakia, eats chicken for breakfast, lunch and tea, and has consumed over 12,000 chickens since the early 1970s.

NOTHING BUT CHEESE
Dave Nunley from Cambridgeshire, England, has eaten nothing but grated mild cheddar cheese for more than 25 years and gets through 108 kg of it every year.

DIET OF WORMS
Wayne Fauser from Sydney, Australia, eats live earthworms.

twist it!

It takes more brainpower to work your thumb than to control your stomach.

Half a million new stomach cells are made by your body every minute!

Whenever you blush, the lining of your stomach gets redder too.

During the course of your life you will produce enough saliva (that's your spit) to fill a swimming pool.

The acids in your stomach are so strong they could dissolve a razor blade!

If you unravelled your oesophagus, stomach and intestines they would reach the height of a three-storey building.

CRAZY

Sonya Thomas is America's competitive eating champion. She weighs just 45 kg, but has managed to put away 46 mince pies in ten minutes and 52 hard-boiled eggs in just five!

EXTREME HEARTBURN

Don't forget to look out for the 'twist it!' column on some pages. Twist the book to find out more fast facts about the bodies we live in.

Hold it Up!

>> bones >>

Let's have a look...

Inside your body there's a gigantic jigsaw puzzle holding you up. Made from up to 300 bones, your skeleton stops you from squelching and slopping all over the floor.

Bones are terrifically tough. In fact, a piece of bone the size of a matchbox is four times tougher than concrete! That's why the most precious body bits are protected by bony armour, such as the skull, rib cage and pelvis.

Bones are living, growing parts of your body and make up around 20% of your weight. If you break – or fracture – a bone, your body will instantly get to work on the repair job, growing new spongy bone in less than two weeks!

AMAZING!

Bone tissue can be spongy or hard. Spongy bone is full of holes, which makes it both incredibly strong and lightweight.

CLEVER!

Some bones contain bone marrow, where blood cells are made.

Skull

Ball and socket joint

Humerus

Vertebra

Sternum

Rib

Ulna

Pelvis

Femur

Fibula

Tibia

Knee joint

Bones don't bend, but they can move; but they meet. These move places where they called joints. connecting are held together by ligaments. joints are tissue called tough

Ripley's Believe It or Not!®

There are **206 bones** in an adult's body. Half of them are in the feet (52) and hands (54). Babies have around 300 soft bones, but some of these join together as the baby grows.

Minerals, such as calcium, make your bones hard. If you sucked all the minerals out of a leg bone, it wouldn't be much stronger than a piece of string.

Your bones are **softer than an adult's**. They won't fully harden until you are 18 years old.

You will probably bend – or flex – your finger joints more than **25 million** times in a lifetime: even more if you play an instrument!

Humans have tail bones. Called the coccyx (say cox-six), this part of your spine helps you lift heavy objects and keep balanced.

Most people have 12 pairs of ribs, making 24 in total. However, one person out of every 500 has 13 or 11 pairs instead!

Twenty years ago amazingly flexible **Ray Gonzales** discovered that he had such flexible joints that he could twist his body 180 degrees so that his feet point completely the wrong way. Great for walking backwards!

DON'T TRY THIS AT HOME!

HOW LOW CAN YOU GO?

Limbo-skating, shown off here by Aniket Chindak from India, involves stretching your ligaments so much that the body can fold almost flat. With enough speed, Aniket can roller skate underneath a parked car!

Use the Force

>> muscles >>

No matter how much you grow, there are parts of your body that shrink – muscles! Thankfully, these bundles of mighty fibres only get smaller to move a bone, before returning to their normal size.

Muscles give you power; they make up half your body weight and provide the pulling forces that allow you to bend an arm or lift a foot. Without your muscles – whether they're feeble or fearsome – you simply wouldn't be able to move. You've got 100 just in your head, face and neck!

Xie Tianzhuang, an 87 year old from China, lifted 14 bricks with his teeth in 2005. The bricks weighed 35 kg altogether.

MOVE IT!

Muscles usually work in pairs. Bend your arm and flex your biceps to see the muscle bulge as it shortens. As you relax your arm the biceps relaxes and the triceps muscle below contracts (becomes shorter).

There are three types of muscle. **Skeletal muscle** helps you move and **smooth muscle** does jobs such as keeping food travelling through your digestive system. **Cardiac muscle** makes your heart pump blood. Skeletal muscles are attached to bones by tough fibres, called tendons.

Bent arm – biceps is contracted.

PUCKER UP!

You use 11 face muscles to frown, 12 to smile and 20 to kiss!

The triceps muscle will contract to straighten the arm again.

Keep on truckin'

The Rev. Jon Bruney, from Indiana, USA, is famous for his strongman achievements, such as bending steel bars and tearing phone directories in half. In 2004 he and two other strongmen joined forces to pull a 15-tonne trailer for 1.5 km.

need a lift?

Need a lift? Ask John Evans – he could possibly carry you and your car on his head! His best effort is balancing a car weighing 160 kg for 33 seconds.

BIG WORD ALERT!

GLUTEUS MAXIMUS
The biggest muscle in your body is called the gluteus maximus. It's in your bottom.

twist it!

Way back in the 1920s performer Clarence Willard of the USA amazed audiences by growing 15 cm in height, just by stretching the muscles of his knees, hips and throat.

The tiniest muscle in the body is called the stirrup. You have one inside each ear, and it is no bigger than this number 1.

Your body is about two-thirds water, and about half of this is contained in your muscles.

Humans have more than 600 muscles in their bodies, but caterpillars have more than 4,000!

Turn your foot outwards and you will be using 13 different muscles in your leg and 20 in the foot. Taking a simple step forwards uses 54 muscles!

MEGA MUSCLES

9

Under Pressure

>>blood >>

Blood: you know it as the oozy red stuff that pours out when you cut yourself. But about 5 litres of this thick liquid is racing around your body, keeping everything in good order. Lose half of your blood and you'll drop dead!

Blood is like a river of life. It carries oxygen and nutrients to every cell, and mops up all the toxic waste. It's also at the front line of your body's defence system. White blood cells track down and kill any nasty bugs that are out to damage, or even destroy, you.

There are five types of white blood cell. They patrol your body on the lookout for bacteria, viruses, cancer cells and other unwanted visitors.

CRUSTY!

Scabs are made up of dried, clotted blood and dead skin cells that stick together making a natural plaster.

Blood is made up of red cells, white cells and fragments of cells called platelets.

Red blood cells use iron to transport oxygen. That's why you need this mineral - found in meat and some vegetables - in your diet.

NUTRIENTS

Substances that provide goodness for growth and health, like fats, proteins, and carbohydrates. One of the roles of blood is to carry nutrients around the body.

Ripley's **Believe It or Not!**®

BLOOD SUCKERS!

Long ago it was believed that people suffering from some illnesses had 'too much blood'. Blood-sucking leeches were used on the skin to suck out the excess!

Artery wall

Red blood cell

Surgeons operating on a man in Vancouver, Canada, in 2007, were used to the sight of blood – but not dark green in colour! Doctors think it turned that colour because of medication the patient was taking.

Plasma

blood is brilliant

* **Bone marrow** makes around 2 million red blood cells every second.

* A single red blood cell can carry about one billion packets of oxygen around your body. You have **25 trillion red blood cells**...so that's a lot of oxygen!

* **One drop** of blood contains around 5 million red blood cells.

* **Blood** can be taken from one human body and put into another, in a life-saving procedure called a transfusion. Frank Loose of Germany has donated some of his own blood more than 800 times, and has saved dozens of lives with his gift.

Blood cells float in a fluid called plasma. Blood makes up about 8% of your body weight.

Take Heart

In the centre of your chest is your heart. It's a powerful, pumping organ that sends blood whizzing around a network of blood vessels at speeds of 270 km a day!

When your heart beats it pumps blood from inside the heart around your body, through blood vessels. In between beats your heart fills with blood again. Your blood carries oxygen to all parts of your body to make them work.

It gets this oxygen from your lungs when you breathe in. This oxygen-rich blood is taken to your heart to be pumped around the body.

When the blood has delivered the oxygen to your body it comes back to the heart to be pumped out again to collect more oxygen from the lungs.

BODY PUMP

A boy called Goga Diasamidze from Tbilisi in Georgia was born with two hearts. The second of them is near his stomach and works perfectly well.

Your heart beats around 60–80 times a minute, but doing exercise can increase this rate to 200 times a minute!

aorta
carries oxygen-rich blood to the body

pulmonary artery
takes blood to the lungs, to collect oxygen

right atrium
blood from the body enters the heart here

left atrium
receives oxygen-rich blood from the lungs

left ventricle
pumps blood to the body through the aorta

right ventricle
pumps the blood to the lungs

blood vessels

There are two types of large blood vessel. Arteries (shown in red) carry blood away from the heart. Veins (shown in blue) carry blood towards the heart. There are both veins and arteries in all parts of the body.

BEAT IT! Your heart will beat more than 3 billion times if you live to old age and will have pumped enough blood to fill an oil tanker 46 times over!

BRRR!

Capillaries are tiny blood vessels. They connect arteries to veins, and make up 98% of the total length of all blood vessels.

Many of 'Ice Man' Wim Hof's amazing feats take place in icy conditions. Here, he stood in 703 kg of ice cubes for an incredible 1 hour 12 minutes! He has mastered the ability to increase his heart rate and the blood flow to his extremities (like his fingers and toes) to stop the cold affecting him as badly.

HEART OF THE MATTER

Blood vessels connect your heart with all your body bits. If you could lay these tubes out in one long line, they would measure 100,000 km and would circle the world more than twice!

At any moment, about 75% of your blood is in your veins, but only 5% is in your capillaries. The remaining 20% is in your arteries.

CORONARY
To do with the heart.

CIRCULATORY
The network of blood vessels and heart - and the way they send blood round and round the body - is called a circulatory system.

13

Seeing is Believing
>> eyes >>

Eyes are jelly-filled cameras and your body's number-one sense organs. All day long your eyes keep your brain busy, passing it masses of information about the world around you.

Rays of light pour into your eyes, where clear lenses focus them to make a crisp, clean image. Nerves zap info about the image to the brain, which has the tricky task of turning those nerve signals into vision. It can even combine the images from both eyes to make a single 3-D picture.

It takes six muscles to move each eyeball, so you can get a good view all around. If you spy something sad, your tears drain into tiny holes in the corner of your eyes, and flow into your nose. That's why your nose runs when you cry!

Lens

Aqueous humour

Pupil

Iris

Cornea

EYE SPY

Human eye muscles move around 10,000 times a day!

Student Jalisa Mae Thompson can pop her eyeballs so far out of their sockets they hardly look real!

14

Vitreous humour

Retina

Optic
nerve

FOR YOUR EYES ONLY

BIG WORD ALERT!

HUMOURS
The aqueous and vitreous humours are clear substances (either watery or like jelly) in the eyeball.

Eyes are delicate organs, so we have eyelids, eyelashes, and tears to protect them.

WOOOOAHHH!

A visual (or optical) illusion tricks us into seeing something that isn't real. Look at this picture, let your eyes roam from circle to circle, and it will appear to have moving parts. Of course, it doesn't, but sometimes your brain can't quite keep up with messages sent by your eyes.

The coloured part of your eye is called the iris. It controls how much light enters the pupil, to produce perfect images, and protects your eyes from sun damage.

Surround Sound

>> ears >>

Listen carefully – it's time to find out how ears hear. These auditory organs don't just help you to sense sound: they stop you from falling over, every time you take a step!

That fleshy flap stuck to the side of your head is just one part of an ear. Each flap, or pinna, sends sound down your ear canal to the eardrum, which vibrates. Those vibrations shimmy through the tiny hammer, anvil and stirrup bones into a shell-shaped organ, called the cochlea.

GET THE BALANCE RIGHT

Squashed next to the cochlea is an organ of balance. It is made up of three tubes, all filled with liquid. If you spin round, that liquid swishes about, making you dizzy!

The cochlea is where the real business of hearing happens. Sound is turned into nerve impulses and sent at lightning speed to the brain. And hey presto – you can hear!

Your smallest bones – stirrups – are in your ears. They measure 2.6 mm long and weigh 0.004 g.

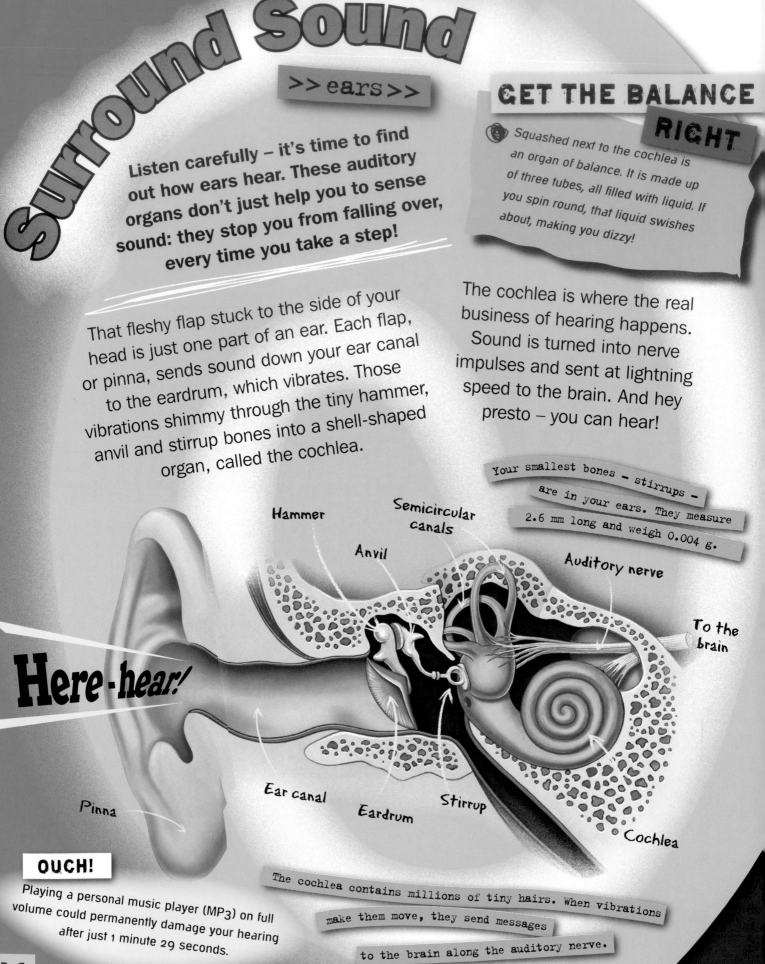

Hammer

Semicircular canals

Anvil

Auditory nerve

To the brain

Here - hear!

Pinna

Ear canal

Eardrum

Stirrup

Cochlea

OUCH!

Playing a personal music player (MP3) on full volume could permanently damage your hearing after just 1 minute 29 seconds.

The cochlea contains millions of tiny hairs. When vibrations make them move, they send messages to the brain along the auditory nerve.

SOUNDS AMAZING

Beethoven was a famous composer of classical music. He continued to write and perform great music even when he lost his hearing!

Wei Mingtang from China has leaky ears. He attaches a hose to them, and then blows out candles or inflates balloons!

Earwax and ear hair protect your ears, and even prevent insects from nesting in the ear canal!

Earwax can be yellow, orange or brown and gross old bits drop out of your ears all the time.

People used to believe that earwigs would climb into ears while people slept, and burrow into their brains to lay their eggs. It's not true, honestly!

twist it!

STEADY AS YOU GO

Balancing on a high wire is tricky enough, but this guy managed to pedal his bike 30 m above the ground without falling off!

BIG WORD ALERT!

AUDITORY
To do with hearing.

It may sound strange (ha ha!) but many people around the world enjoy performing feats of 'ear strength'. This man, celebrating Chinese New Year in Beijing, is just one of several choosing to pull vehicles along with his ear. Ouch!

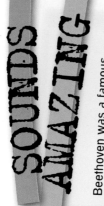

Hey, you've got something in your ear! Narayan Rasad Pal of India proudly shows off the long strands of hair that grow from his ears. They measure an incredible 10 cm!

Staggering Senses

>> taste, touch and more! >>

Close your eyes and touch the tip of your nose with a finger. Easy isn't it? But how did you know where your nose is? Thanks to your staggering senses you've got up-to-date nuggets of info whizzing to your brain all of the time.

How many senses do you have? People used to say we have five: we can see, hear, touch, smell and taste. But now we know there are loads more. Feelings such as cold and hunger are all part of your body's sensory world.

RUMBLE!

Got tummy rumbles and pain in your belly? Your body is telling you to eat – now! You could make like Japan's Takeru Kobayashi, international champion hot-dog eater. In 2005 he retained his title by eating 49 hot dogs in 12 minutes. His personal best is an unbelievable 53.5 hot dogs in that time!

BRRR!

Getting so cold it hurts? Time to put on your winter woollies or go somewhere warm, before you freeze to death. Ice swimmer Lewis Pugh swam 1 km in the Antarctic wearing only a swimming cap, goggles and trunks, in a temperature of 0°C. He was in the water for 18 minutes 10 seconds and described the feeling as a 'screaming pain all over his body'.

FASCINATING FACT

The makers of Stilton cheese have launched their own perfume with the same smell!

Your brain collects sensory information from the rest of your body – and tells you how to react to it all.

FASCINATING FACT

It takes just 0.02 of a second for your brain to realise when you've dropped a book on your toe.

YUM!

Taste is an important sense – it can warn you that something isn't good for you to put in your mouth.

FASCINATING FACT

An ice-cream parlour in Nice, France, offers its customers up to 70 different flavours of ice cream, including tomato and basil, black olive, and chewing gum!

Your senses are there to tell your brain what is going on inside, and outside, the body.

Your brain then knows if things are changing, and can decide when to make your body react – perhaps to keep you safe, or get some food or drink, for example.

The information is sent to your brain along nerves.

Some pains keep you from harm or tell you it's time to visit the doctor. Not so for Miss Electra, who had 2 million volts of electricity passed through her body and out of her fingertips for a TV show in Hollywood. She doesn't feel any pain when this takes place!

OUCH!

SNIFF!

Pongs and stenches tell us to stay away – whiffy food might be covered in nasty bacteria. Mind you, blue cheese such as Stilton smells strong but is safe to eat. The blue veins are mould caused by bacteria, and if you think they smell like stinky feet, you'd be right – it can be the same bacteria.

OOPS!

Stumbling, tripping and falling over – it happens to us all, but most of the time your body is great at keeping your limbs in the right place, and balanced. Shame it only goes wrong when everyone is looking!

Open Up!

Your mouth is home to 10,000 taste buds, up to 32 teeth and billions of bacteria. In fact, there are more bacteria in your mouth than there are people on the planet!

A mouth is a dark hole with lots of jobs to do, from chewing and crunching to coughing, swallowing, tasting and talking. Food begins its digestive journey in your mouth, where teeth grind it into little pieces and morsels get juiced up with sloppy saliva. Thanks to the taste buds on your tongue you can sense flavours – such as salty, sour, sweet and bitter – and either enjoy your snack-attack, or choose to spit out yukky bits.

Dentine

Tough white enamel

Pulp (contains nerves and blood vessels)

Gum

Root

INSIDE A TOOTH

Lips

Incisor

BABY TEETH
Your teeth started growing about six months before you were born!

Gum

Uvula

Tonsil

Tongue

Molar

Premolar

Canine

KEY FACTS

There are more than **500 types of bacteria** in your mouth. Most of them are helpful bugs, but the bad ones can rot your teeth or give you stinky breath.

You use your jaws, lips and tongue to speak. Babies' first sounds include **'coo', 'ba ba' and 'da da'**.

Girls are usually better at identifying flavours than boys, but boys prefer stronger flavours than girls. Teenagers don't like sour-tasting food!

tongue twister

Mohammed Rafi doesn't just roll his tongue, he can sculpt it into all sorts of shapes. He can even roll it inside out by flipping the whole thing backwards!

SALIVA

Spit! The gooey substance made by your mouth – in fact, your mouth produces about 1 litre of the stuff every day. Eeoogh!

LONG LICK

Annika Irmler from Germany has a tongue that measures 70 mm. It is so long that she can lick ice cream from the bottom of an ice-cream cone.

Ripley's **Believe It or Not!**®

TOOTH ART

These tiny tattoos of famous people have been done on teeth!

TOOTHY GRIN

Babies are usually born with no teeth, although it isn't rare for a newborn to have one or two. Sean Keeney from England was born in 1990 with 12 of his teeth already!

TASTY!

Stephen Taylor from the UK has a 9.5-cm tongue – long enough to touch his nose AND to lick his own nostrils!

It's Alimentary

>>digestion>>

Your digestive system is a fabulous food processor. It pulps and pulverises food before squirting it with burning acids and churning it into a stinking stomach soup that is forced through your gurgling guts (also known as intestines).

Billions of bacteria break the food down into smaller and smaller bits so they can be used to fuel your body and help it grow.

A sandwich's journey through your alimentary canal – from mouth to anus – can take more than 24 hours and covers around 7 m in total.

The small intestine is lined with tiny, finger-like villi. On the surface of the villi are even tinier folds called microvilli. If you stretched all your villi out they would cover an entire football field!

KEY FACTS

* Your **alimentary canal** is packed with chemicals called enzymes. These powerful juices help break food down into useful nutrients.

* The **oesophagus** is a tube that leads from your mouth to your stomach. It's made of muscles that force the food downwards.

* Your **gall bladder** and **pancreas** store and produce substances that help the body's digestive process.

* After a big meal your stomach can stretch to **40 times** the size it was when it was empty.

* One type of bacteria – *Heliobacter pylori* – survives in the stomach's burning juices. These mini-bugs infect half of the world's people, and can cause pain and ulcers.

Oesophagus

Stomach

Pancreas

Gall bladder

Appendix

Anus

Small intestine (ileum)

Large intestine (colon)

LIVE SCORPIONS

Father-of-two Hasip Kaya of Turkey has been addicted to eating live scorpions since he was a boy.

FLY FEAST

In protest at his town's garbage collection service, a man named Farook, from Tirunelveli, India, started eating nothing but flies.

LIVE TREE FROGS AND RATS

For over 40 years, Jiang Musheng of China has eaten live tree frogs and rats to ward off abdominal pains.

CHICKEN FEED

Jan Csovary, from Prievidza, Slovakia, eats chicken for breakfast, lunch and tea, and has consumed over 12,000 chickens since the early 1970s.

NOTHING BUT CHEESE

Dave Nunley from Cambridgeshire, England, has eaten nothing but grated mild cheddar cheese for more than 25 years and gets through 108 kg of it every year.

DIET OF WORMS

Wayne Fauser from Sydney, Australia, eats live earthworms.

Michel Lotito

ate bicycles, televisions, and even aircraft with no problems! He had to take them apart and slurp down mineral oil before swallowing the smaller bits.

DON'T TRY THIS AT HOME!

Sonya Thomas is America's competitive eating champion. She weighs just 45 kg, but has managed to put away 46 mince pies in ten minutes and 52 hard-boiled eggs in just five!

EXTREME HEARTBURN FORMULA

MAALOX 3

twist it!

It takes more brainpower to work your thumb than to control your stomach.

Half a million new stomach cells are made by your body every minute!

Whenever you blush, the lining of your stomach gets redder too.

During the course of your life you will produce enough saliva (that's your spit) to fill a swimming pool.

The acids in your stomach are so strong they could dissolve a razor blade!

If you unravelled your oesophagus, stomach and intestines they would reach the height of a three-storey building.

CRAZY

what a Waste

As your food makes its way through your digestive system, your body makes sure that nothing it needs goes to waste. A team of friendly organs slogs away, like a recycling plant, to suck out every last bit of goodness.

Blood vessels carry the nutrients from your food to the liver, where they are sorted, processed, recycled or stored. The rubbish bits are sent packing back to your guts where they join the leftovers to make the solid stuff that leaves your body. It's called faeces (say fee-sees).

Faeces is made up of old blood cells, bits of undigested food, bacteria and water. The liquid waste is called urine and it's actually 96% water.

aorta
A giant blood vessel that carries oxygen-rich blood to the organs of the body.

inferior vena cava
A blood vessel that takes oxygen-poor blood back to the heart.

two kidneys
These work like filters to sort out toxic waste and remove it. They also send unwanted water to the bladder.

liver
The largest organ inside the body and, with your guts, helps to sort out the good from the waste.

ureters
Long tubes that pass liquid waste from the kidneys to the bladder.

bladder
Holds urine until it's time to let it out.

urethra
Tube that takes urine from the bladder to outside the body.

TIME FOR TEA

A restaurant in Kaohsiung, China, is totally toilet themed – diners sit on toilets, eat at basin-style tables, and have their food served in bowls shaped like toilets or waste pots.

CLEAN MACHINE!

This wacky flying machine was part of a 2003 flying demonstration in France. Don't flush while you're up there!

FEELING FLUSHED!

Fancy finding a snake in your toilet! A 3-m-long boa constrictor appeared in a loo in Manchester, England, and then again in a neighbour's toilet bowl after moving through the sewage system of a block of apartments.

twist it!

FUNNY TUMMY

Sloppy poo is called diarrhoea (say die-ar-ee-ah). It's often caused by nasty bugs – so wash your hands before eating and after using the loo!

Your liver is the second largest organ of your body and it can continue to work if 80% of it is removed. It will even grow back to its previous size!

One person produces enough urine to fill about 270 bathtubs during a lifetime.

Many ancient people believed that drinking their own urine would cure tummy troubles or other digestive disorders. Romans used it in their toothpaste.

Even waste is recycled. Faeces and urine travel from toilets through sewage pipes to sewage plants, where waste matter can be turned into fabulous fertilizer to be spread on farmers' fields.

WASTE PRODUCTS

There are more than one million tiny tubes, or filters, in the kidneys. They are called nephrons and measure around 65 km in total length!

KEY FACTS

→ The liver has more than 500 different jobs, including cleaning blood, storing vitamins and preparing nutrients to be used by the body.

→ If you don't drink enough water your kidneys stop water going into your bladder. That makes your wee look darker.

→ Minerals in urine can turn into solid stones, called bladder stones, which have to be removed by a doctor.

Life's a Gas

>> breathing >>

Oxygen: you can't see it, smell it, touch it or taste it – but without this gas your body would pack up in minutes. Thanks to your lungs you can concentrate on other stuff while you breathe in oxygen – more than 10 million times every year!

Lungs are lazy life-savers. With no muscles of their own, these air-filled puffers rely on rib muscles and a diaphragm to work. Every breath you take draws air into your lungs, which are each packed with 300 million alveoli. These thin-skinned sacs are swap shops, where oxygen is traded for carbon dioxide, the waste gas you breathe out.

Phew!

With six billion people breathing in oxygen you may expect we'd run out one day. Fortunately, when green plants respire they use up carbon dioxide, and produce oxygen. Phew!

Air-mazing

Air contains 21% oxygen. Breathing pure oxygen is actually dangerous.

look inside your lungs!

BREATHE OUT

BREATHE IN

Bronchi

Trachea

Bronchus

Bronchioles

At the top of the trachea is a voice box, or larynx. Passing air through the larynx as you breathe out makes your vocal cords vibrate, creating sound. Breathing in and talking at the same time is almost impossible – try it!

Left lung

Right lung

Bronchiole

Artery from heart

Deoxygenated blood from heart

Oxygenated blood to heart

Alveoli

RESPIRATION

Breathing in and out. All the body bits that get oxygen from the air, and pass it into the blood stream, are called the respiratory system.

BIG WORD ALERT!

DEEP BREATH

You breathe around 20 times a minute — that's 700 million times during an average lifetime.

Every day you breathe in enough air to fill 1,000 party balloons. (But we don't recommend it!)

Your lungs contain around 300,000 capillaries (tiny blood vessels). If they were stretched out they would measure 2,400 km!

twist it!

The loudest scream ever measured was 129 decibels — that's loud enough to make your ears hurt.

In June 2008, freediver Herbert Nitsch from Austria used just the air in his lungs to sink to a record-breaking 214 m in the ocean. During the dive, which took 4 minutes 24 seconds, his lungs shrank to the size of a fist and filled with blood, returning to normal at the surface.

David Merlini spent 10 minutes 17 seconds chained and handcuffed underwater in 2007, without air. He escaped from the five sets of handcuffs and 27 kg of chains all without taking a single breath.

27

Under Command

Electrical messages buzz around your body at speeds of 100 m/second – that's ten times faster than the fastest human has ever run, and about one-third of the speed of sound.

These speedy signals whizz backwards and forwards on the body's super-highways – your nerves – and are controlled by the brain. You've got a lot of nerve: if all of your body's nerves were spread end to end they would measure more than 150,000 km!

Nerves instruct muscles to move, and send back messages to the brain about what's happening to your body. Like a bossy headteacher, they have everything under their command.

Toddlers and teenagers have far more neurons (nerve cells) than adults or kids of other ages.

Axon

nervous twitch?

A thick nerve cable – the spinal cord – runs up through the centre of your spine to your brain. It's kept safe and snug inside a column of backbones.

Muscle fibre

Junction between nerve cell and muscle

Nerve cell

Nerves are like long cables of electrical wire. They are made up of nerve cells, called neurons.

Your brain and all your nerves together make up the nervous system. This is your body's main command and control centre.

LOOK OUT!

Catch! Entertainer Nathan Zorchak lives on his nerves, juggling with three chainsaws whizzing past his nose!

STEADY!

You want quick reactions? Look no further than Australian Anthony Kelly, who can catch flying arrows and – wearing a blindfold – speeding paintballs!

SNAKE KISSER

In Malaysia in 2006, Shahimi Abdul Hamid kissed a wild, venomous king cobra 51 times in three minutes, using his quick reflexes to dodge bites from the 5-m snake.

ON YOUR NERVES

If you burn your hand, your nerves swing into action, instructing your muscles to move it to safety in just 0.01 seconds.

The longest cells in your body are found in your brain. Stretched out, each one would measure up to 10 m long.

Professor Kevin Warwick studies robot technology. He has had silicon chips inserted into his body, which connect his nervous system to a computer. Now he can control doors and lights without lifting a finger!

twist it!

NOT FUNNY

The nerves in your elbow run close to the skin, which is why a knock to your 'funny bone' feels so weird.

Uncover your Cover

>> skin >>

No thicker than 20 pages of this book, yet making up 16% of your weight, your skin works hard for your body!

Here are just some of its jobs: it stops your body soaking up water like a sponge, prevents your blood from boiling or freezing, keeps bugs and bacteria out of your insides, and even senses pain and touch. But that's not all: 50 million bacteria call your skin home!

Skin is the body's largest organ and a piece no larger than a postage stamp holds 650 sweat glands, 20 blood vessels and 1,000 nerve endings.

DON'T BE BLUE!

Except Paul Karason can't help it. His skin has turned blue after treating a skin complaint with an ointment containing silver. He has also been drinking 'colloidal silver' for about 15 years, which may have helped with his colour change. It might even have turned his insides blue, too!

GROSS!

A million dust mites live in your mattress and pillow. They feed on the dead skin cells that fall off your body at night.

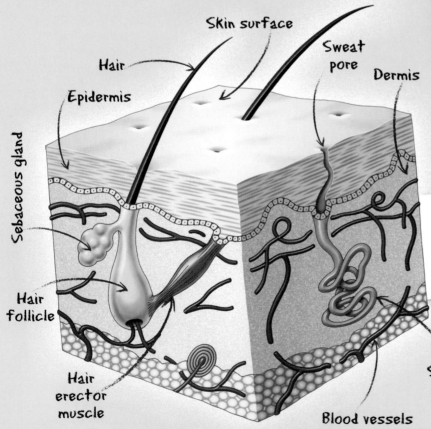

- Skin surface
- Sweat pore
- Dermis
- Hair
- Epidermis
- Sebaceous gland
- Hair follicle
- Hair erector muscle
- Blood vessels
- Sweat gland

Sweat glands in your skin help to control temperature. When you are hot they ooze sweat, which is 99% water and 1% salt. As sweat evaporates, or dries, it cools your skin.

Meet the Leopard Man of Skye! The skin of Tom Leppard from Scotland has been tattooed with the markings of the big cat; over 99% of his skin is tattooed, with only the insides of his ears and the bits between his toes having no artwork.

The top layer of your skin is called the epidermis. It is made from dead cells that are shed every 27 days.

Stretch it!

Gary Stretch has a rare skin condition that allows him to stretch it – and stretch it – and stretch it some more. His skin cells are affected so they don't hold together as tightly as they should, and his skin appears very loose on parts of his body.

Twist it!

Lady Gray Rosemary Jacobs of the USA has grey skin. She thinks the change of colour happened after she used nose drops, which contained tiny amounts of the metal silver.

A computer mouse has been invented that can sense people's emotions. By measuring changes in the user's skin, such as sweat and temperature, the mouse can tell if he or she is feeling sad, angry or tired.

If you could peel off an adult's skin and stretch it out on the floor it would measure around 1.5 to 2 sq m and weigh as much as 4 kg.

Feet sweat because there are 250,000 pores (tiny holes) in the soles. Each squirts about 12 teaspoons of sweat a day.

SKINNY FACTS

Hair-raising Tales

Hair today, gone tomorrow! Most of your body is covered in strands of hair, which grow at a snail's pace of just 8 mm a month. After a few years, each strand of hair falls out.

Thankfully, new hairs grow from special cells in your skin, called follicles, all the time. Each follicle can make about 20 new hairs in a lifetime. Hair grows fastest in the summer, but those dozy follicles like to slow down during the night and catch some ZZZZ. Both hair and nails are made from dead cells that are toughened with a protein called keratin, which is surprisingly stretchy.

Testing 1-2-3
Scientists can use one strand of hair to find out a person's age, sex and race.

BIG HAIR!
Aaron Studham sports a magnificent Mohawk hairstyle that reaches 53 cm in height. It takes him an hour – and lots of hairspray – to get the look.

ITCHY
Tran van Hay from Vietnam has not cut his hair for 38 years and it now measures a staggering 6.2 m. He wears it coiled around his head, which keeps the hair neat and tidy, and his head warm.

KEY FACTS

→ You could live without hair or nails, but they are useful. Hair helps to keep you warm, and nails protect your delicate fingertips from damage – and are dead handy when you have an itch!

→ You have hair all over your body except on the palms of your hands, the soles of your feet and your lips. Humans have as many hairs as chimpanzees!

→ Blonde, brunette, raven-haired or redhead? You get your hair colour thanks to the skin pigment, melanin.

snip-its and cuttings

👁 Human hair was used to make soy sauce in some Chinese barber shops, until the government banned it!

👁 Your toenails contain traces of gold!

👁 Mats made from human hair were used in San Francisco to mop up oil that had leaked into the San Francisco Bay.

👁 Blonde people have about 130,000 hairs on their heads. People with red, black or brown hair have up to 40,000 fewer.

HAIR FACE

Larry Gomez was born with a very rare medical condition, which causes thick, dark hair to grow all over his face and body.

SCRATCHY!

Lee Redmond has been growing her fingernails since 1979. She said it was tough trying to open doors or get dressed, but was very proud when her talons reached 84 cm! Sadly, Lee was involved in a car crash in 2009 and her nails all broke off.

Speedy
Fingernails grow about four times faster than toenails.

Grow Up!

>> from birth onwards >>

In about 270 days, or 38 weeks, a single cell can grow into a perfect human baby!

At birth the baby weighs around 3.4 kg and measures a mere 50 cm from head to toe – but will increase in weight a massive ten times by the age of ten. From ten to 20 this blooming baby will double in weight and should reach around 1.7 m tall.

ALL CHANGE

The time of growth, when kids develop into adults, is called puberty.

TINY TOT

Babies are supposed to develop inside their mother's womb for 37 to 40 weeks, but tiny Amillia Sonja Taylor was born after only 21 weeks and 6 days. She was only 24 cm long.

Heave!

Two-year-old Salvador Quini, from Argentina, could lift weights heavier than himself – not so much a strongman as a strongboy!

SUPER BABY!

Mexican newborn Antonio Cruz weighed a massive 6.4 kg when he was born – about twice the weight of many new babies. Look how big he is compared to the average-sized baby lying next to him!

MARVELOUS MIRACLE!

day 1

Size of a fullstop

6 weeks

Size of a lentil

10 weeks

Size of a strawberry

16 weeks

Size of a pear

Ageing is a one-way road, which eventually leads to death. Most people can expect to live into their seventies, although there are some supercentenarians (aged over 110 years) alive today.

George Blair – or 'Banana George' to his friends – is the world's oldest barefoot waterskiier. Age hasn't stopped him trying new challenges: he learned to snowboard when he was 75, drove his first racing car aged 81, and made his first parachute jump at 82!

ALL AGES

Three babies are born into the world every second.

Babies born on the island of Bali are not normally named until they are three months old. Before then, they are all called 'mouse'!

Souleymane Mamam of Toga was just 13 years old when he played a World Cup qualifier match against Zambia.

Thanks to the body's amazing ability to heal and grow, doctors are able to stitch new body parts on to people, including arms and faces. Hearts, lungs and kidneys can also be transplanted.

'Red' Rountree was 80 years old when he first decided to rob a bank in the USA. He carried on with his life of crime until he was 92, when he was finally locked up in prison!

twist it!

38 weeks

The baby is developed and ready to be born in the next few days or weeks.

30 weeks

The baby can now hear its mother talking.

22 weeks

The baby can open and close its eyes, and has eyelashes.

Circle of life...

The time from birth to death and the way that humans reproduce (have babies) is called a life cycle.

35

Do people with big noses smell more? Better ask Mehmet Ozyurek – his huge honker from Turkey – an impressive measures 8.8 cm.

No way!

The Long and Short of it

>>all shapes and sizes>>

Breaking news! When it comes to bodies, none of us is 100% 'normal'. The simple fact is every one of us is unique – different and totally special.

From big noses to big toes and bulgy brains to bulgy biceps, your body grows by following a set of rules laid down by your DNA. Found in every cell of your body, DNA is a code for life that's packed with between 20,000 and 30,000 instructions, called genes.

How you turn out isn't just down to DNA though; it's about environment too. That means that the way you choose to live your life will affect your body, mind and health.

Bao Xishun looks down on everyone he meets, because he is one of the tallest men in the world, reaching 2.36 m. Bao had a growth spurt when he was 16, which lasted for seven years. Each of Bao's legs is about 1.5 m long!

He Pingping was unusually small, reaching just 74.61 cm in height. From Mongolia, he was the size of an adult's palm when born. His condition was caused by a change in the genes that control growth.

DOWNSIZING

When humans lose weight their fat cells don't disappear, they just get smaller.

Guddi from India is just 97 cm tall. Despite her tiny size, Guddi gave birth to a baby measuring 50 cm.

SUPER SPIRAL

- There is so much DNA in one human-body cell that, if you could stretch it out, it would measure 2 m.

- Everyone gets two lots of DNA, one from their mother and one from their father.

- You can inherit features, such as the colour of your hair or eyes, from your parents. The information is carried in the DNA. That's why people usually look like other members of their family.

- Unusually tall or short people may have DNA that has been damaged, or changed. Sometimes, they just inherit their height from their parents.

37

Mind Reading

>> inside your head >>

Brains are always busy, controlling every body bit including your circulatory system, digestive system, nervous system, senses and feelings.

Your brain is like a lump of warm jelly to touch, but don't be fooled by its cunning disguise. This unbelievable organ contains the very essence of you: your thoughts, dreams, memories, hopes and desires. It's home to your amazing, incredible, magical mind!

Every brain is wrapped in a bony case called a skull, which protects its 100+ billion cells. These cells can handle more than 86 million bits of information a day and your memory can hold at least 100 trillion facts during your lifetime – which is the same as a 1,000 gigabyte computer!

This bit deals with movement.

The front of the brain is in charge of personality, thinking and behaviour.

The brain is divided into different areas with different jobs to do. For example, there are particular areas that control speech, movement, vision and hearing.

This is where the brain works on sight and hearing.

This bit controls sleep and growth.

This area controls balance and coordination.

This is where the brain identifies sounds.

Spinal cord

Stephen Wiltshire has an incredible talent for drawing and can produce remarkably accurate and detailed pictures solely from memory. In 2001, after flying in a helicopter over London, he drew in three hours an aerial illustration of a ten-square-km area of the city, featuring 12 landmarks and 200 other buildings, all in perfect perspective and scale.

These brain cells help to feed and repair the brain. They are shaped like stars.

Everybody can boost their brain's brilliance by reading, learning, playing and exercising. Eating a healthy diet helps too.

Dominic O'Brien has won the World Memory Championships eight times. In 2002 he memorised 54 packs of shuffled cards and remembered each card – all 2,808 of them – in almost perfect order. It took more than four hours to recite them, and he made just eight mistakes!

A bit mental!

A brain weighs about 1.4 kg but if all the water it contains were squeezed out, it would weigh just 283 g!

Unborn babies grow new brain cells at the rate of 250,000 every minute!

For its size, a brain needs up to ten times more energy to work than any other organ.

The brain is one of the few body parts that cannot carry out any movements at all, since it has no muscle tissue.

There is no feeling in the human brain, only in the membrane surrounding it, which contains veins, arteries, and nerves. So a person would feel no pain from an injury to the brain alone.

At the age of 60 a person's brain holds four times more information than it did at the age of 21.

Lights Out

>>sleep>>

Your eyelids are drooping, your arms and legs feel heavy, and you know it's time to get some shut-eye. Sleep is nature's way of giving all those hard-working body bits of yours some well-earned rest.

The good news is that when the thinking part of your brain hits the snooze button, the other parts that control important jobs – like breathing – stay wide awake!

Most people spend around one third of their lives asleep. Some of that time is spent in a deep sleep, but some of it is also spent dreaming. If you're unlucky, a few of those dreams may turn to nightmares!

LIGHT ON YOUR FEET

Shh! Don't wake your family when you need to get up in the middle of the night – wear these slippers with torches in the toes and you can see where you're going without banging into things!

You've been sitting still, doing very little, when the urge to yawn suddenly takes over. It's your body's way of getting more oxygen into your lungs, so you are ready for action.

NAP ATTACK

The longest anyone has survived without sleep is 18 days, 21 hours and 40 minutes. The woeful wide awaker suffered from memory loss and hallucinations (that means seeing imaginary things).

New parents lose between 400 and 750 hours of sleep in the first year of their baby's life.

Teenagers and young children need about ten hours of sleep a night.

Snails can sleep for long periods of time – up to three years!

Stephen Hearn crashed his car at 113 km/h when he was sleepwalking near Birmingham, England. When he was found, he was in his pyjamas and still snoring.

Sleepwalker Lee Hadwin of North Wales is a good artist when he is asleep, but when awake he struggles to draw at all! Wandering round the house in his sleep he draws everywhere – even on walls and tables!

twist it!

WAY TO GLOW!

A pillow with a built-in light allows its users to read in bed and also acts as an alarm clock. The light can be set to come on gradually at the time you want to wake up. The increasing lightness acts like a sunrise and wakes up sleepyheads in a more natural way than the blare of an alarm or radio.

Your brain needs sleep to be able to work properly. Without sleep you'd find it hard to think clearly, remember anything or keep yourself safe.

SOMNAMBULISTS

It's not unusual for people – especially children – to walk or talk in their sleep. Sleepwalkers are called somnambulists.

ANIMALS SLEEP TOO

Pythons sleep for around 18 hours out of 24, but sheep only need about four hours of sleep.

ICE HOTEL!!

Fancy sleeping on an ice bed? You can do this in Shimukappu, Japan, where an ice hotel caters for sleeping, eating and bathing – all on ice.

Zzzz

SHUT-EYE!

Your eyelids close when you are feeling drowsy. When you dream your eyeballs flick from side to side.

SNORE!

The back of your mouth and throat relax and may partly block your airways, leading to that pig-snuffle snoring sound!

GROW!

While you snooze your body can repair itself and put spare energy into growing.

DREAM!

No one really knows why we dream, but it may help us to organise our thoughts and remember stuff.

RELAX!

Your muscles relax. When you dream, the ability to move your limbs is (usually) switched off – which stops you from acting out your dreams. If this doesn't happen you may find yourself sleepwalking.

41

Under Attack

You may not know it, but your body is engaged in a deadly battle with the world, right now! It's true – there are plenty of bugs, bacteria and other baddies out there, just waiting to do you harm.

Thankfully, the human body has evolved over millions of years to repel most invaders. Your body has an amazing ability to defend itself, and even repair damage done to it. Without this ability even a simple cold could spell the end of you. Of course, we can't always do it alone, so it's time to say a big 'thank you' to doctors!

Your body fights attackers 24/7. From your tough outer layer – skin – to spit, strong stomach juices, bacteria in your gut, hair in your nose and tears in your eyes, there are lots of clever defence systems in place.

BIG WORD ALERT!

IMMUNE SYSTEM

Your body has an immune system, which makes white blood cells that attack and kill invaders, such as the virus that causes flu.

BUG ALERT!

A VIRUS ATTACKS THE BLOOD STREAM!

Vomiting, sneezing, crying, spitting, coughing and diarrhoea (runny faeces) are all ways of chucking out stuff your body doesn't like.

TASTY!
These tiny fish nibble at dead skin on customers' feet at a spa resort in Japan – and leave the feet clean and refreshed!

TOASTY!
Stand back! This fire treatment is popular in China to help prevent colds and flu.

MUDDY!
It's a mucky business in these mud baths, which are meant to ease pain and diseases.

KILL OR CURE

In ancient times, headaches and other medical problems were sometimes cured by drilling holes into the skull. Known as 'trepanation' this operation is still carried out in some parts of the world today.

Maggots are sometimes used to treat infected skin and tissues, which they eat. Because they don't eat healthy fesh, these greedy grubs help wounds to heal before life-threatening infections, such as gangrene, can set in.

A pair of spiders set up home inside the ear canal of nine-year-old Jesse Courtney from America. Thankfully, doctors were able to extract the eight-legged invaders, and no harm was done.

Over 2,000 years ago, Hippocrates, a doctor, told his patients to chew on bark from a willow tree when they were in pain. We now use an ingredient found in willow bark to make aspirin!

twist it!

OLD BONES
In some Chinese villages, dinosaur bones are ground up to make a paste. It's used to treat dizziness and leg cramps!

Muntoyib, an Indonesian bee-sting therapist, covers himself with hundreds of live honeybees in India. Some people think that bee venom injected from live stinging bees helps treat chronic pain.

in the olden days

Before modern medical science took over, people invented some weird ways to get better.

CATCH THAT SHREW!
Aching bones were treated with the help of a dead shrew. Sufferers were told to keep the furry little creatures in their pockets.

DON'T BE AN ASS!
Passing a child under the belly of a donkey three times was said to cure whooping cough.

HOT AND STEAMING!
If you had TB – a deadly chest disease – you'd be told to kill a cow, stick your head into its warm body, and breathe in deeply.

TOM FOR YOUR TUM!
One of the first types of tomato ketchup was used to cure diarrhoea in the 1800s.

Fit for Life
>>take care>>

There's no such thing as a perfect human, but keeping your body bits in tip-top shape has got to make good sense.

The human body is like a mighty machine with lots of working parts. It needs to be taken care of – and that means exercise and a good diet. There are around six billion humans on the planet, and many of them, from super-sized sumo wrestlers to bendy-bodied yogis, keep the power switch turned to maximum.

For kids, it's easy to keep it fun. All you've got to do is play, eat well and sleep. But for some groaning grown-ups, it's a hard, sweaty slog keeping those muscles and bones in peak condition.

GULP!

Water makes up 60% of your body weight. It's the liquid of life, so drink up. Your bones and teeth are packed with calcium – there's loads of this mighty mineral in milk.

GRUB!

Veggies and fruit are great grub. At least one-third of a human's diet should be made up of these super foods.

GO FOR IT!

Squash – the hard-hitting racquet and ball game – has been voted the healthiest sport ever, beating running, swimming and basketball into first place.

FITNESS FUN

Hula hooping is a hu-lotta fun! Alesya Goulevich spun 100 hula hoops at the same time, at the Big Apple Circus in Boston in 2004.

SURF'S UP!

Surfers are super-fit because they use almost every muscle in their bodies to stay balanced and upright on their boards.

PUSHING IT

Ashrita Furman, a health-food store manager from New York City, is super fit. Amongst his amazing feats are climbing Mount Fuji on a pogo stick, hula hooping with a 4.46-m hoop, and doing 9,628 sit ups in an hour. Here, he's pushing an orange along for one mile using his nose!

twist it!

Kids should be exercising for at least 60 minutes every day. Running, walking, cycling and playing sports all keep you fit for life.

You're never too young to get fit! In 2006 1,100 babies took part in a crawling marathon. The mini racers had to crawl along a 5-m track, and the young winner was rewarded with a bag of baby goodies!

Aged 91, Ervin Ashley of the USA climbed 2,000 steps every day to keep in shape!

Cycling backwards is a popular sport in some parts of the world. Riders sit on the handlebars and pedal in reverse.

Tirtha Kumar Phani from India ran more than 60 km every day, for one year. He clocked up a blistering 22,581 km in total!

FITNESS FANATICS

stick with it!

Kyle Nolte from Arkansas has got so good at jumping on his pogo stick, he can also play baseball, hula hoop or skip whilst pogoing!

HUMAN BODY INDEX

47

ACKNOWLEDGEMENTS

COVER (l) © Sebastian Kaulitzki – istockphoto.com, (r) Lilli Strauss/AP/PA Photos; **2** (r) Raymond w. Gonzales, (t/l) © Peter Galbraith – fotolia.com; **4** © Sebastian Kaulitzki – istockphoto.com; **5** (t/r) Lilli Strauss/AP/PA Photos; **6–7** (dp) © AlienCat – fotolia.com; **7** (b/l) Raymond W Gonzales, (b/r) Simon De Trey-White/ Barcroft Media; **8** (r) © Peter Galbraith – fotolia.com, (l) © AlienCat – fotolia.com; **9** (l, b) ChinaFotoPress/Photocome/PA Photos; **10** (sp) © V. Yakobchuk – fotolia.com; **11** (c) © Sebastian Kaulitzki – istockphoto.com, (r) © Wong Sze Fei – fotolia. com; **13** (l) © Roman Dekan – fotolia.com, (t/r) AP Photo/Rubin Museum of Art, Diane Bondareff, (b/r) Jeff Chen/Trigger images; **15** (b/r) © saginbay – fotolia.com; **14–15** (b) © Xtremer – fotolia.com, (c) © saginbay – fotolia.com; **17** (l) Patrick Hertzog/AFP/Getty Images, (c) Prakash Hatvalne/AP/PA Photos, (r) Reuters/Christina Hu; **18** (t/l) Reuters/ Seth Wenig, (b/l) Camera Press/Terje Eggum/Scanpix; **18–19** (b/c) © ktsdesign – fotolia.com; **21** (l) Manichi Rafi, (b) Steven Heward/toothartist.com, (t/r) Fabian Bimmer/AP/PA Photos; **22** (l) Dr. Kessel & Dr. Kardon/Tissues & Organs/ Getty Images, (b) Reuters/Staff Photographer; **23** (t/r) Nils Jorgensen/Rex Features, (b) Matt Cardy/Getty Images, (b/r) Stan Honda/AFP/Getty Images; **24–25** (c) © Mark Kostich – istockphoto.com; **25** (c/r) Sipa Press/Rex Features, (b/r) Phil Noble/PA Archive/PA Photos, (t/r) Reuters/STR New; **27** (l) Dan Burton/underwaterimages.co.uk, (t/r) John Bavosi/Science Photo Library, (b/r) Gabriel Bouys/AFP/Getty Images; **28** (l) © Sebastian Kaulitzki – fotolia.com; **29** (l) Roger Bamber/Rex Features, (r) Tim Barnsley/Armidale Express; **30** (r) NBCUPhotobank/Rex Features; **31** (t) Ian Waldie/Rex Features, (r) Scott Barbour/Getty Images; **32** (l) Jean/Empics Entertainment, (r) Thanh Nien Newspaper/AP/PA Photos; **33** (l) Rex Features, (r) Tao-Chuan Yeh/AFP/Getty Images; **34** (r) Reuters/Ho New; **35** (l) Reuters/Victor Ruiz, (r) George A. Blair; **36–37** (dp) Reuters/China Daily China Daily Information Corp; **36** (t/l) IHA/UPPA/Photoshot; **37** (l) © Dmitry Sunagatov – fotolia.com, (t) © Sasha Radosavljevic – istockphoto.com; **39** (t) Gary Bishop/Rex Features, (b) Greg Williams/Rex Features, (r) © Sebastian Kaulitzki – fotolia.com; **40–41** (dp) © Veronika Vasilyuk – fotolia.com; **40** (c) Rex Features; **41** (t/r) Solent News/Rex Features, (b) Reuters/ Kim Kyung Hoon; **42** (sp) © David Marchal – istockphoto.com; **43** (t/l) Reuters/Larry Downing, (t/c) Chu Yongzhi/ ChinaFotoPress/GettyImages, (t/r) Reuters/China Daily China Daily Information Corp – CDIC, (b) Reuters/Beawiharta Beawiharta; **44–45** (b) Reuters/Sergio Moraes; **44** (t) Boston Herald/Rex Features; **45** (l) Reuters/Shannon Stapleton

Key: t = top, b = bottom, c = centre, l = left, r = right, sp = single page, dp = double page, bgd = background

All other photos are from Ripley Entertainment Inc.

All artwork by Janet Baker & Julian Baker (JB Illustrations)

Every attempt has been made to acknowledge correctly and contact copyright holders and we apologise in advance for any unintentional errors or omissions, which will be corrected in future editions.